EPONA

HOGAN

YELLOW-STONE PARK
CODY
WYOMING
ROCKY MOUNTAINS
Fort Laramie
Buffalo Bill's Grave
DENVER
PIKES PEAK
Gold
COLORADO

MISSOURI

NEBRASKA

PLATTE RIVER

RIVER

OREGON TRAIL

Geographic
Center of U.S.

Pony Express

ROME

KANSAS RIVER

KANSAS

Buffalo Bill
born in Iowa
1846

Fort Leavenworth where
Bill grew up

ISBN 978-0-9643803-7-0

Published by Beautiful Feet Books
1306 Mill Street
San Luis Obispo, CA 93401

www.bfbooks.com
800.889.1978

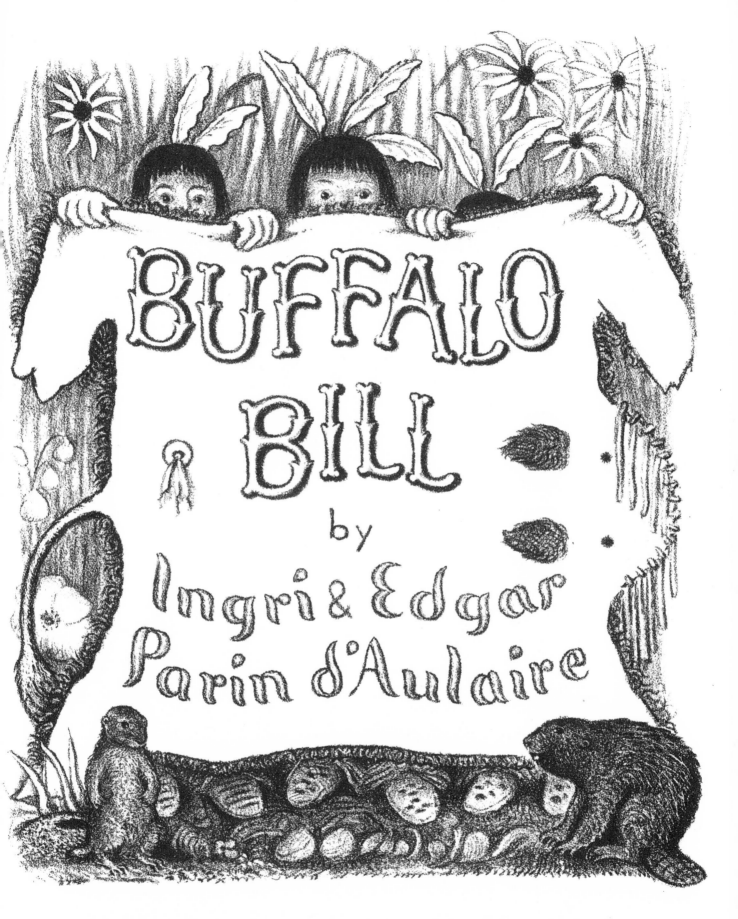

BUFFALO BILL

by
Ingri & Edgar Parin d'Aulaire

Beautiful Feet Books, San Luis Obispo, California

In the far-off days when Buffalo Bill was a boy the land west of the Missouri River still belonged to the Indians. Like a vast ocean of grass, the great plains stretched ever westward. There millions of buffaloes grazed and the Indians could hunt as much as they wished and still the herds did not grow smaller. Indian hunters, on swift ponies, rode after the herds or sneaked up on them disguised as buffaloes themselves. Jealously the Indians guarded their hunting grounds and fought the white men who came in covered wagons from farms and bustling towns east of the Missouri River.

Bill grew up at the edge of the plains, in the wilds of Kansas Territory. There his father had settled with his family to trade with the friendly Kickapoo Indians. Little Bill Cody did not go to school, and he could neither read nor write. But early he learned to aim and shoot his father's gun. His father had taught him that, until law and order came, a frontier boy must be able to look after himself. His home was far from white neighbors, but Bill was not lonely. Right by his door went a bumpy road, cut through the grass by the wheels of the wagons that crossed the plains. It was called the Oregon Trail. Sometimes a trader with Indian trinkets or trappers with bundles of precious furs came riding down the Oregon Trail and stopped to tell of their adventures. All through spring covered wagons with emigrants for the far West would stop at his door. Wide-eyed children would stare at Bill from under the canvas cover while their fathers asked about the dangers ahead. And ever so often a string of heavy ox-drawn wagons, loaded with freight and supplies for the West, lumbered by.

The drivers of the wagons, the lusty bullwhackers, were singing and bragging and telling tall tales of Indian battles and buffalo hunts. They loved the plains and their adventures. When Bill was big he

would be a plainsman and a bullwhacker too! Bill's playmates were
Kickapoo Indian children. He frolicked and romped and hunted small
game with them, and learned their games and their language.

He traded his brand-new buckskin suit for a little wild Indian pony,
and so he had a horse of his own.

Sometimes he rode bareback, Indian-fashion,

sometimes he rode with a saddle,

and soon he rode as if he and the horse were one.

Before he was twelve he rode so well that he got himself a grown
man's job with a train of ox-drawn wagons bound across the plains
with cattle and supplies. First rode the wagon boss, scanning the land
for signs of danger. Then came the bullwackers, cracking their long
whips so they could be heard for miles. Last came young Bill, riding in
the dust, keeping the cattle together. All day long they rumbled along.

At night they made camp, sat around the fire, sang and told stories. Then they all rolled up in their blankets and went to sleep. The stillness was broken only by loud snores and howling coyotes. Life on the plains was wonderful, thought Bill.

Day after day they traveled ever farther west. Soon the plains were
dotted with big, shaggy buffaloes. Bill went hunting with the men and
for supper that night they had buffalo humps roasted over the bon-
fires. That was the best food Bill had ever tasted. He loved buffalo
hunting but it was a dangerous sport for when startled a whole herd
rushed off blindly with a thundering of hoofs and a clattering of horns.
They ran over each other and over everything that came in their way.
One day the wagon train was in the way of a stampeding herd and Bill
was swept along. Courageously he hung on to his horse and let it run
with the buffaloes until he could safely wind his way out of the throng.
But it took days to repair the smashed wagons.

Buffalo country was hostile Indian country too. The hoot of an owl,
the howl of a wolf, might mean Indians on the warpath.

One moonlit night Bill spied an Indian aiming his arrow at one of the bullwhackers. Quick as a flash he raised his gun and shot the Indian first. After that the other plainsmen treated Bill like a grown-up man. Their Bill was the youngest Indian fighter on the plains, they boasted. Wild Bill Hickok became Bill's special friend. He was the fastest man on the trigger in the whole Wild West. He could shoot on the updraw, with two hands at once, faster than another man could reach for his gun. With him for a teacher Bill became one of the best shots on the plains.

And good shots were needed. For an Indian brave could shoot ten of his poisoned arrows while a white man stopped to reload his gun. When a band of yelling Indians came charging across the flat prairie, the plainsmen drew their wagons into a circle and hid behind them.

The wagons studded with quivering arrows soon looked like porcupines, but in their shelter the white men could shoot and reload their guns. When the Indians saw what crack shots they had for foes they gave up and galloped off as fast as they had come.

Bill made many trips across the plains and became a seasoned plains-man. Sometimes he and his wagon train had to turn back. Sometimes they got all the way to Fort Laramie. There the United States flag was waving proudly against the blue haze of the Rocky Mountains, and the travelers could rest while the soldiers kept watch. There Bill met Kit Carson, the most famous of all the great scouts of the West. He had led many scouting expeditions all the way to California. Keen-eyed Kit Carson took a liking to young Bill Cody, who worshiped him in return. He taught Bill to read the language of the plains. Each broken blade of grass, each stirring bush, had a message for those who could understand it.

Bill learned to spell out nature's hidden language, but words and letters he still could not read. At nearby Register Cliff he stood with shame and watched while the travelers from the covered wagons scratched their names on the rock. Little boys and girls could write. He could sign his name only with a cross. There was no way around. He had to get off his horse and sit on the school bench instead. And so, at last, he learned his A B C's. But as soon as he could write his name with a flourish, he was off for the wide-open spaces again. Now he signed up with the Pony Express.

Eighty-six young daredevil riders were hired to carry news and mail across plains and mountains. All along the westward trail a chain of stations was built, well stocked with fodder and fast ponies. The riders galloped from station to station. Bill was the youngest of them all. Swift as the wind he galloped off, the precious mail pouch over his saddle. At the end of his run another rider waited. Bill threw the mail to him and he sped off. In this way hard-riding boys and sweating ponies carried the mail in nine days from the Missouri to the Pacific.

But it happened sometimes that Bill found his station in ashes, the men killed by Indians, the ponies driven off. Then he must ride his tired pony on to the next station, dodging Indian arrows on the way. Once he rode more than three-hundred miles in one stretch.

Outlaws, too, were a danger, but they never caught Bill unprepared. One day two masked bandits jumped out from a hiding place. One seized his pony's head, the other its tail. "Reach for the sky! Hand over the mail pouch," they growled. Meekly Bill made as if to mind, but suddenly both robbers founds themselves on the ground. The one was felled by his flying mail pouch, the other one knocked down by his rearing horse. Before they had recovered their sense, Bill was far away, the precious mail safely hidden under his saddle.

While the riders of the Pony Express were speeding across mountains and plains, other men were struggling to put up telegraph wires across the country. Indians burned the poles, and buffaloes rubbed their backs against them until they toppled over. But new poles came up, and when Bill and his friends had been riding for two years, the line was completed. Almost before a pony could be saddled, the telegraph wires had carried the news from coast to coast. The days of the Pony Express were over.

This was at the time when the Civil War was raging in the United States. The people in Kansas wanted no slaves, and Bill and the other boys marched off to the East to fight. Bill was now a young man, and he made a handsome soldier. He got himself a little wife, as soldiers are apt to do, but he could not stay contented away from the wide-open spaces of the West. And when the war was over he returned to Kansas with his wife. Now he had a family to support, and for a while he drove a stagecoach. That was fun and well paid too. He swung his whip and soared across the plains. He grew a long mustache and a short goatee and let his hair fall down over his shoulders. That was to tease the Indians who would never get that handsome scalp, he said. As in the old days, clouds raced over the endless sky, and prairie dogs came scurrying out of their burrows to scold intruders and scramble into their holes again. But the wilderness of Bill's childhood had changed. Kansas had now become a state, and more and more people were moving in.

Puffing little trains were eating their way through the grass, ever deeper into the plains. In front of them were buffalo herds and whooping Indians, but in their wake were farms and bustling towns.

In vain Bill tried to race the steaming engines. He laughed in glee when buffaloes blocked the tracks, for then the train had to stop, however much the engine puffed and whistled.

Bill saw the railroaders getting rich selling lots for towns wherever a station was built. "I'll build a town and get rich myself," he thought. So he got himself a piece of land straight out ahead of the railroad tracks. He divided the land into squares and laid out streets on the prairie grass. He called the place Rome, and he talked so boastingly about what a fine town this Rome would be that people came from far and near and started building their houses. When the tracks came in they would pay for their lots. Bill felt like a millionaire.

And the railroad tracks were built to the town - right through the town - and right on beyond! The railroaders planned no station in Rome. They wanted to sell their own land. So, a few miles away they built a depot. "Gentlemen, this is the site of your town," they called. "Come, buy our lots, we'll move you here for nothing." Every soul pulled up and moved. There stood Bill, as poor as before, but the railroaders were still richer.

29

"I didn't hit gold this time," thought Bill, "but I still have my horse and my gun." And the railroaders, for all their money, were hungry for meat. Juicy buffalo steaks were good, but hostile Indians watched over the buffalo herds, eager to scalp white hunters. Bill was sure no Indian could ever catch him. His horse was so fast and so well trained, Bill only had to whisper into its ear and it would do his bidding. He would hunt buffalo for the railroaders, and so great a hunter was he that he kept more than a thousand men supplied with meat. The rail-roaders paid him handsomely and boasted there wasn't a hunter like him on the plains. They called him Buffalo Bill. That was a name to Bill's liking.

But there was another Bill on the plains who also answered to the name of Buffalo Bill. Both Buffalo Bills were big hunters and they decided to hunt together one day and see who was the best. The one who lost would be just plain Bill again. Bill Cody was so sure of himself, he rode bareback to give his rival a better chance. His horse knew just what to do. It ran in front of a buffalo herd and put itself in position so Bill could shoot. The horse would let him miss one shot, but if he ever missed twice, it galloped off to another buffalo. When the buffaloes were counted, Bill had shot almost half again as many as his rival. From then on he was the one and only Buffalo Bill.

31

But with growing fury the Indians looked at the white men who were taking their land and killing off their buffalo herds. Soon Indian war drums sounded all over the plains. Soldiers were sent out to protect the white men and drive the Indians off their ancient hunting grounds. Buffalo Bill was sorry for the Indians. But he knew that, vast as the plains were, there wasn't room for Indians and white men both. And as he knew the plains better than most other white men, he became an army scout. The soldiers thought as much of him as the railroaders had. He was full of cheer and good stories. He was seldom tired and never afraid. When nobody else dared ride with warnings to outlying forts, he rode alone. He tied himself to his horse so he wouldn't lose his mount if it stumbled into a prairie-dog hole in the dark and sent him flying. Without his horse a man was badly off on the plains.

One day, when Buffalo Bill was riding an ornery government mule, he alighted to drink from a stream and dropped the rein for a second. Right away the mule made off. Bill tried to catch it, but in vain.

When he ran, the mule ran. When he walked, the mule walked too, just ahead of him. So Bill ran and he walked and he walked and he ran for thirty miles, while the mule looked back at him with a smirk.

Fortunately for Buffalo Bill he met no Indians that day.

Even Buffalo Bill could lose his mount. But he never lost his way in the wilderness when he led the soldiers in pursuit of dodging Indians. His trained eyes saw each quiver of the sagebrush, each broken blade of grass. Where he led the way in his white buckskin suit, the soldiers followed. In fighting, too, he charged on ahead with arrows flying about his head. One day an arrow went straight through his hat. But Buffalo Bill had luck on his side. The arrow only scratched his scalp.

One tribe after another was rounded up and sent off to reservations.
Soon the last hostile Indian was forced to move toward the setting sun.

Before long settlers were plowing their fields where buffalo once had roamed. Law and order had come to Kansas. But Buffalo Bill was bored. One day as he dozed in the shade under a wagon, wondering what to do now, a shiny boot nudged him awake.

"Aha," said the fat little man to whom the boot belonged, "so you are as handsome as they say you are brave. If you'll tell me your adventures, I'll write them in books and make you famous." That suited Buffalo Bill just fine. He liked very much telling tall tales about his adventures, and the little fat man was a very fast writer. Soon people all over the country were reading dime novels about Buffalo Bill and his amazing adventures, and wanted to see their hero in person. He went East to the big cities, he traveled North, he traveled South. He looked so brave and so handsome in his wide-brimmed hat and his snow-white buckskin suit that people came from far and near to look at him. They paid much money to see him shoot his gun and do his Wild West stunts. Buffalo Bill had hit gold. He went home and talked some of his hard-shooting, rough-riding friends from the plains into coming with him. He rounded up some Indians, too, and started a show of his own.

All over the United States - yes, even in Europe - people cheered when Buffalo Bill and his Wild West Show came to town. Children and grown-ups, plain people, lords and kings thronged to watch whooping Indians race their ponies in pursuit of stagecoaches and covered

wagons. Then, in a cloud of sawdust, gallant and handsome Buffalo Bill, followed by his Wild West riders, came to the rescue. They always arrived in the nick of time, there was no end to their daring. The Indians were shot, to appear again, as fierce as ever, in the next act.

For forty years Buffalo Bill traveled all over with his show. He, more than any other man, made the world aware of the romantic Wild West and the wonderful new lands west of the Missouri. He grew famous and rich, but still he could not stay contented for long away from the wide-open spaces of home. Home to him did not mean only the gently rolling hillocks in Kansas where his father's humble cabin stood, but all the vast expanse of the plains and mountains where he had roamed in his youth.

High up in Wyoming he built himself a fine ranch where his wife and his children could live in comfort. And there, not far from Yellowstone Park, he helped to found the beautiful town of Cody, named in his honor. Kansas, Nebraska, Wyoming, Colorado all vied with each other in claiming him as one of their own.

Buffalo Bill grew old, but as long as he lived his gun hand was steady and he and his horse still seemed to be one. He never grew tired of telling his tales of the days of his youth when the Wild West was wild. And when he died, old and full of years, he had chosen for himself as his last resting place the top of a mountain in Colorado, overlooking the plains he had loved so much.

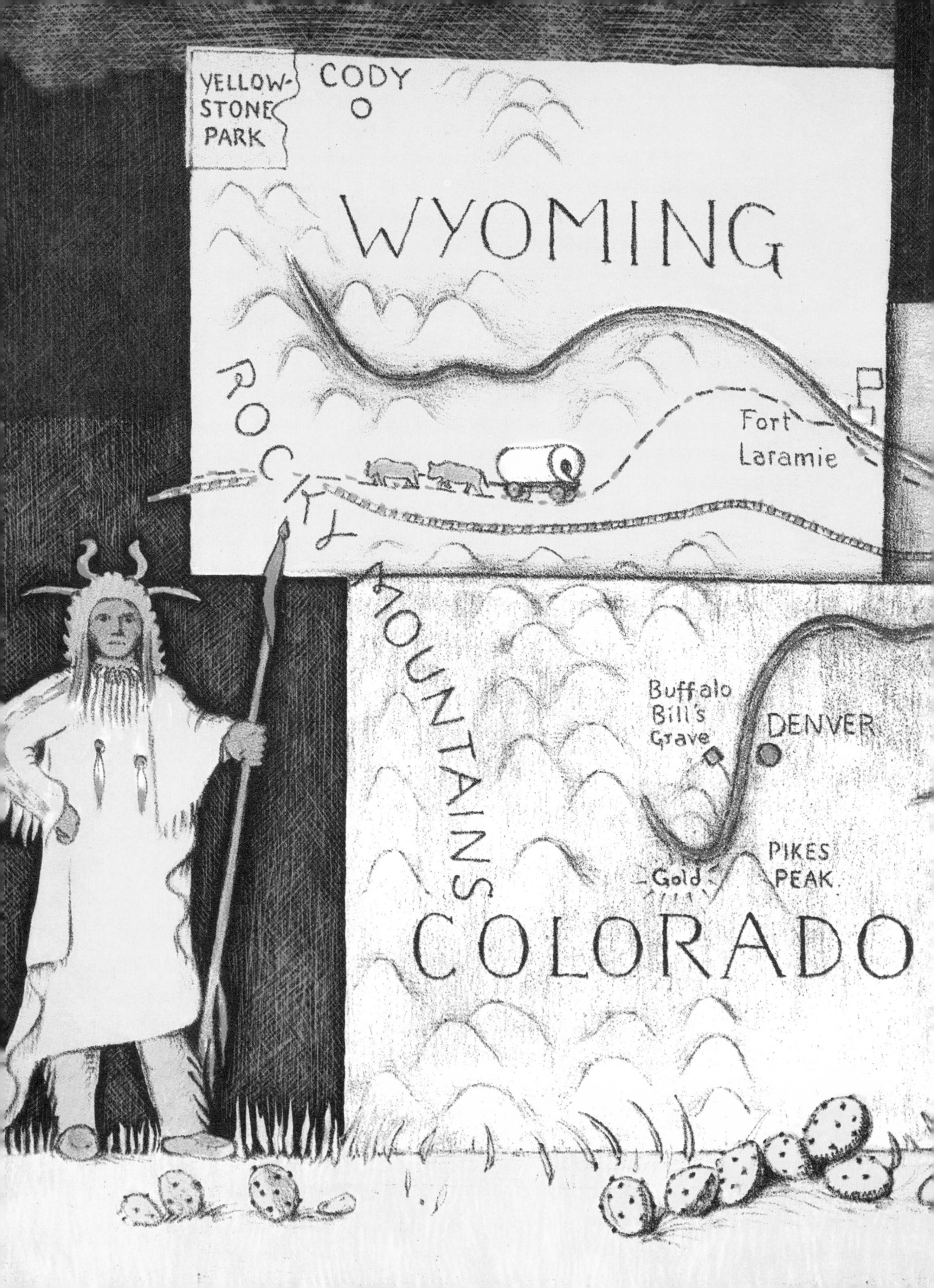
YELLOW-
STONE
PARK
CODY
WYOMING
ROCKY MOUNTAINS
Fort
Laramie
Buffalo
Bill's
Grave
DENVER
Gold
PIKES
PEAK
COLORADO

MISSOURI

NEBRASKA

OREGON TRAIL

PLATTE RIVER

RIVER

Geographic
Center of U.S.

Buffalo Bill
born in Iowa
1846

Pony Express

ROME

KANSAS RIVER

Fort Leavenworth where
Bill grew up

KANSAS